LIFESTYLE SERIES

Y0-CKO-062

How to Get the Job You Want

Written by Robert L. Iles
Edited by National Seminars Publications

NATIONAL SEMINARS PUBLICATIONS
6901 West 63rd Street • P.O. Box 2949 • Shawnee Mission, Kansas 66201-1349
1-800-258-7246 • 1-913-432-7757

How to Get the Job You Want
Published by National Seminars Publications
© 1989 National Seminars Publications

All rights reserved. No part of this publication may be reproduced or utilized in any form by any means, electronic or mechanical including photocopying, recording or by any information storage and retrieval systems, without permission in writing from National Seminars Publications.

Printed in the United States of America

1   2   3   4   5   6   7   8   9   10

ISBN 1-55852-027-9

Table of Contents

A Systematic Approach to Finding the Right Job............1

How to Put Together a Good Resume......................7

How to Write a Good Cover Letter......................23

Interviews: How to Get Them and Conduct Them...........29

Tips on Filling Out an Application Form.................39

How to Stretch Your Money to the Max..................45

How to Handle the Stress of Job Hunting..................49

1
A Systematic Approach To Finding The Right Job

Job Hunting Is a Job

Those people who are the most successful in getting the jobs they want do not approach the process of finding a job casually. They *work* at job hunting.

Obviously, the amount of time you can devote to job hunting depends on whether you are unemployed or still working at your current job while trying to find a new one. If you aren't working, then job hunting has to become your full-time job. If you are working, then you need to devote a specific number of hours each week to this process. Regardless of your situation, the key elements in job hunting are:

- Know what type of job you want.
- Organize your approach to job hunting.
- Do something each day that contributes to your job search.

Decide What Job You Want

You can't find the right job if you can't describe it, at least broadly. Many people waste a lot of time and energy responding to ads for jobs that "look interesting," "sound like fun," or that they think will make them money quickly. Avoid wasting time by defining:

- The things you do well.
- The things you enjoy doing.
- The things that you have experience doing.

Also write down elements of a job that would be unacceptable. They might include:

- Working evenings, nights or weekends.
- Extensive travel.
- Working on a straight commission or other specialized compensation system.
- Relocating to another city.

Then define your ideal job. This does not necessarily have to be the job you are most qualified for, given your current skills and experience. However, if your ideal job requires a radical career change, your planning should include a strategy for gaining some experience in your newly chosen field and/or figuring out how your experience could be an asset in this area.

Some people can't define their ideal job. They can tell you what they like to do and what they've done well in the past, but they can't synthesize this into a specific job definition. If you fall into this category, don't despair. Your greatest problem is that you might waste time applying for jobs that you don't have a chance of getting but which caught your eye because they involved a task you enjoy.

Describe your ideal job as best you can, then use the description as a way of evaluating each job opening. Before you apply for a job you should be able to answer the following questions:

- Do I have the minimum skills required for this job?
- Do I have the minimum number of years' experience required?
- Do I meet the education requirements? If not, could my experience reasonably substitute for some of the education required?

- Does this job represent a step up from my current (or last) position, a lateral move or a step down?
- How does the salary range (if stated) fit in with my salary history and requirements?
- Does it involve any of my unacceptable job elements?

This preliminary evaluation will prevent you from applying for jobs that you are either over-qualified for, under-qualified for, that would be a bad career move, or that you might reject because of low salary or unacceptable working conditions.

Organizing Your Job Hunt

One of the key things that will determine your success in job hunting is your ability to get organized and stay organized. This means that you plan each day and week around activities that will help you get the job you want. Some of these activities include:

- Reading classifieds in the newspaper, business publications and professional or trade magazines.
- Sending out resumes and cover letters in response to advertisements.
- Meeting with prospective employers.
- Sending follow-up letters to prospective employers after an interview.
- Writing to and phoning friends and business acquaintances to let them know the type of job you are looking for.
- Attending meetings of professional or trade groups in your field.

You Are Job Hunting, Not on Vacation

If you are not working and job hunting, it is vitally important that you avoid acting like you are on vacation. Keep a regular schedule. This means setting the alarm, Monday through Friday, and getting up at the same time you did when you were working. Work at job hunting during normal working hours (8:30 a.m.—5 p.m.) with time out for lunch and several short breaks. Many people can treat job hunting more like a regular job if they get up, dress for work and then leave the house and make phone calls, write letters, and so forth. If you are fortunate enough to have office space you can use, take advantage of it. If you have to conduct your job hunt from your home, make it clear that you are not to be disturbed during specific periods. This is sometimes difficult for you and your family, but as much as possible, try to maintain a businesslike schedule when you are job hunting.

Use a Daily and Weekly Planner

If you set up a *written* schedule of what you will do each day, you'll be more effective.

On the weekly planner shown on the next page are some ideas for the typical job hunter. Use the ideas that apply to you, then add your own to make a daily and weekly plan that fits your needs. Write in the squares what you need to do and when, then pin or tape the schedule up near the phone or your desk. Check off each step as you carry out your plan. Resist the tendency to do things simply whenever you think of them. If you accomplish something every day, you'll feel better and others will see you as a working, methodical person. Conversely, if you won't make the effort to plan or commit yourself to a plan, you are sending the message that you aren't ready to work.

WEEKLY PLANNER

Sunday	Monday	Tuesday	Wednesday	Thursday	Friday	Saturday
Read classified want ads.	Make five phone calls to friends, business colleagues. ——— Send resumes to jobs advertised in Sunday classifieds.	Ask friends to recommend two employment agencies. ——— Have lunch with business acquaintance. ——— Select a set of employment goals in short-term future.	Review personal budget and expenses. ——— Plan weekend recreation.	Follow up on Monday phone calls to get new leads. ——— Get at least two appointments for interviews.	Follow up on resumes sent Monday to jobs advertised in Sunday classifieds. ——— Contact employment agencies.	Consult with insurance person or banker on local employment situation.

2
How To Put Together A Good Resume

What Is the Purpose of a Resume?

In most cases, a resume is supposed to get you an interview, not get you the job. Keep that in mind and you'll write a better one.

If a resume were supposed to get you a job, you could skip the interviews, the application forms, the medical exams and all the other steps job hunters ordinarily go through. You'd just write a good one, sit back and wait for an employer to call and say, "Great resume. You're hired."

Getting a job is a lot like selling something. In this case, your skills, experience and knowledge are the product. Your resume is one way you sell yourself. Like selling anything else, getting the job you want involves several steps:

- Create interest among prospective employers (the customers) through your resume and cover letter.
- Tell how you will benefit the prospective employer's company during the interview (sell the product).
- Demonstrate your skills/knowledge (the product's benefits)

if you are asked to take a pre-employment test.
- You get a job offer (the customer wants to buy).
- You negotiate salary and benefits (define the value of the product and negotiate the price). These negotiations can include time off in the first few months; relocation assistance; a company car; an early salary review.
- You agree on terms and join the organization (the product is sold).

Writing a good resume only helps start the process. It doesn't end it.

Can a Resume Help You Get a Promotion?

In many organizations, the boss or the personnel recruiter pulls resumes from the file when a promotion opens up. For example, sales representatives' resumes might be read when a home office job opens up in sales training or sales promotion. Safety instructors' resumes might be pulled when openings in security occur. Line executives and recruiters use the resumes to remind themselves of the strengths and interests of employees. So you have a lot to gain if you update yours when you:

- Finish a business course or workshop directly related to the organization's products, services or your job.
- Get a college degree, an advanced degree or gain certification for new or enhanced skills.
- Win an award for work performance.
- Successfully manage or help carry out a project that has high visibility, measurable results or is of importance to your company.
- Reach maturity in your present position, that is, run your job smoothly for whatever period of time it takes to show you can handle the challenges.
- Decide on a new career path.
- Hear of interesting new ventures by your company.

Just the act of sending an updated resume helps. It reminds recipients of you, your skills and your career interests. Send a cover letter or memo saying why you are sending the resume just as you would to a prospective employer.

What Goes on a Resume?

That question was asked of a group of 200 recruiters who go to college campuses looking for potential employees and 25 college teachers of business communications.

Here's what they said they expect to see on a resume: job (or career) objectives, employment history and educational history.

Fewer than one-fourth wanted to know anything about pastime activities, participation in organizations, references and personal accomplishments.

Another survey was carried out among the chief personnel officers of **Fortune** 500 companies. They were given a long list of statements about resumes and asked if they agreed or disagreed with them. They strongly agreed with the following statements about what should go on a resume, what a resume should look like and how you should use a resume:

1. Work experience—List jobs held, dates of employment, company addresses, reasons for leaving. (98 percent agreed.)
2. The prospective employee should take a copy of his or her resume to the job interview. (97 percent agreed.)
3. Keeping a resume neat and accurate (no misspellings, no typographical errors) is essential. (96 percent agreed.)
4. Give general and specific educational qualifications, such as majors, minors, degrees. (95 percent agreed.)

What statements did they *not agree* with?

1. Resumes should be three pages long. (Only four percent agreed with that.)
2. Your social life ought to be covered. (Only three percent agreed strongly, 26 percent had "moderate agreement.")

Bear in mind that the first survey was done among college recruiters and college teachers. These responders were no doubt thinking of advice they would give to young people who were wanting to join relatively large companies at the entry level. The top personnel officers were probably thinking of both old and young applicants all across the spectrum of jobs, from high to low.

Put These Things on Your Resume

1. Your name, address and telephone number.
2. Your career objective.
3. Your education. Include honors, scholarships, awards, election to or membership in select societies such as Phi Beta Kappa.
4. Work experience.
5. References are optional. Employers who want them will ask for them on their application form or during an interview.

What Shouldn't Go on a Resume

1. Your hobbies. (Unless they are directly related to your work.)
2. Your marriage status or a family sketch.
3. Your present or your desired salary.

Why Shouldn't I State Salary Needed?

In the survey of top personnel officers, more than half wanted applicants to write their salary requirements on their resumes. That would serve them well, but what about you, the applicant? Before you say how much you expect, you'd like to know the salary range, wouldn't you? Why say you'll take a certain amount when the pay range for the job is several thousand dollars higher? If possible, avoid writing down your salary history or an expected salary. You are giving up a lot of negotiating power if you do. Save that topic for the *interview*. If pressed, you might be able to call and ask what the pay range is before writing down your expected pay or find out the salary ranges for comparable positions at other companies.

Some employment advisers go so far as to suggest you write on the application form, "I'm sure your salary range is reasonable and competitive." Those advisers say you should give salary information when you are in a conversation and can hope for true negotiation.

You have to be the judge of what is best in your particular situation. But keep in mind that you're not likely to get what you want unless you ask for it.

The Most Common Resume Errors

1. Poor appearance. Sloppy typing, misspelled words, uneven margins, irregular spacing, absence of headings.
2. Too lengthy. Keep it two pages or less except in the most unusual circumstances. If you need more than two pages, consider writing a two-page resume that has attached pages for details or extensive lists.
3. Too short. Not enough information, particularly in describing what your duties were on various jobs. Sometimes a job title is enough, but if you have any doubt whether it is, go ahead and tell the reader what your duties were.
4. Unnecessary, irrelevant information. ("Divorced. Like deep sea fishing. A Giants fan. Have traveled to India.")
5. Sending the same resume to all prospective employers regardless of the particular needs of the situation. A petroleum company that needs a chemical engineer isn't interested in the same things about you as a chemical firm that seeks a sales engineer. Tailor your resume to the position you seek.
6. Putting a date on your resume. (Why reveal that it is six months old if the content is still appropriate?)
7. Leaving out important directory information—your address, weekend or evening phone numbers, your name. (Yes, some people do forget to put their name on their resume.)

The Law and Resumes

Various state laws forbid employers to ask for photos. Many

states also have laws against asking you to list:
- Age
- Ancestry
- National origin
- Race
- Religion

If you put such information on your resume, prospective employers may avoid talking to you for fear they will appear to be practicing discrimination.

Four Different Types of Resumes

The *Chronological*, or time-ordered, is the most commonly used resume. The format makes it easy to show how you have spent all your time since starting in the work world, and employers find it easy to read.

The Chronological resume is done in reverse time-order—most recent work first, then the work just prior to that, then the work prior to that and so on. If your education goes much beyond one college degree, consider using the reverse-time order for that, too. If you have a college degree, don't list your high school education.

A disadvantage of the Chronological resume is that most employers' application forms request the very same information. You may therefore say the same things twice and miss the chance to tell what is really special about yourself.

Other types of resumes are designed to bring out the special things about you. The *Accomplishments* resume is what you would likely use when you have been in your work long enough to have a record of success. In an Accomplishments resume, you put emphasis on numbers, facts—anything that is objective evidence of success. Increases in sales dollars, decreases in expenses, higher productivity, lower employee turnover and greater percentages of repeat orders are all examples.

The *Special Skills* resume may be right for you when you have mastered several parts of a job or have completed training that prepares you for more responsibility. Mechanical skills, budgeting skills, communicating skills and managing skills, for example, should be written about. Very often, the person who is ready for promotion but hasn't yet received one should write a

Special Skills resume. Also, the person who has been sent to company-sponsored workshops or to college classes should consider writing a Special Skills resume.

The *Functions* resume is often the best for the unrecognized person. Probably the job title reveals very little about how important the work is. Workers whose titles end in "coordinator" may be in this category. They should describe accurately which pieces of work they carried out for their boss, such as "Gathered and checked all common stock registrations. Had errors corrected by persons responsible for them. Filed report with Securities and Exchange Commission."

You'll find examples of each type of resume on the following pages and information on how to choose one that's best for you in the **Questions & Answers** section following the examples.

If you choose to write an Accomplishments, Special Skills or Functions resume, be *sure* to include an employment summary so the employer can see where you have spent your working time. Nearly every employer wants at least a listing of your work history on your resume. The employment summary can go at the end of your resume and can look like this:

Employment   **1983-present:** Assistant Manager, Joffer, Inc.,
Summary   Welever Ave., St. Louis 63101.

1980-1983: Production Supervisor, Smalley Co., 9771 Pike Blvd., St. Louis 63121.

1976-1980: Production Worker, Smalley Co., Plant 4, Pegasus Park, St. Louis 63129.

The first page of a Chronological Resume.

RESUME

James M. Brook
748 Presidio Ave.
Tovia, MA 02855
Phone: (days) 816-555-5000, ext. 1869
(evenings and weekends) 913-555-7472

Career Objective: Purchasing management in the health care industry.

Education: Bachelor's (1966) and master's (1970) of biology degrees from University of Maine; minor in business administration.

Elected to scholastic honor society.

Employment History:

1978 to present: Purchasing agent for Hemple Laboratories, Kansas City, MO. I buy laboratory equipment and supplies, work with eight science department directors to plan yearly budgets of $6 million or more. The work requires being up-to-date on latest laser and chromatographic sampling techniques.

1968—1978: Junior buyer for Golden Laboratories, Syracuse, NY. Bought laboratory supplies and animal feed amounting to $4 million per year. Worked with laboratory and animal care specialists to set specifications, examined invoices, monitored vendor payments. Promoted from assistant lab director to junior buyer because I helped save 14 percent on lab expenses.

1967—1968: Assistant production manager, Palmer Foods, Hector, MO. Supervised four others directly, helped improve safety and sanitation, planned budgets.

(Employment History continued on next page.)

The first page of an Accomplishments Resume.

RESUME

James M. Brook
748 Presidio Ave.
Tovia, MA 02855
Phone: (days) 816-555-5000, ext. 1869
(evenings and weekends) 913-555-7472

Career Objective: Purchasing management in the health care industry.

Education: Bachelor's (1966) and master's (1970) of biology degrees from the University of Maine; minor in business administration.

Elected to scholastic honor society.

Special
Accomplishments: Designed and implemented new purchasing system. Hemple Laboratories of Kansas City, MO, had bought two smaller companies and was beginning an expansion program when I was hired as Purchasing Agent in 1978. In 14 months, two other company directors and I designed and implemented new procedures for setting specifications, selecting vendors for competitive bidding, examining invoices and verifying payments at headquarters and other company locations (Montana, Ohio and Florida).

Increased volume, decreased expense. As Assistant Lab Director for Golden Laboratories, Syracuse, NY, I revised purchasing procedures for laboratory supplies and animal feed that had been costing $4 million per year. Working with animal care specialists and laboratory personnel, I helped set new specifications, established new invoice-checking procedure and payment monitoring. In the first 12 months, $560,000 was saved (14 percent). The system was adopted company-wide at savings not yet announced. Promoted to Junior Buyer.

(Employment Summary given on next page.)

The first page of a Special Skills Resume.

RESUME

Wilson B. Lane
104 Drury St.
Bether, KY 86061
Phone: (days) 816-555-5000, ext. 1869
(evenings and weekends) 913-555-7472

Career Objective: Laundry and Housekeeping Manager.

Education: High school diploma (1980); seminars on Loss Prevention, Employee Safety, Cardiopulmonary Resuscitation.

Special Skills: Management Skills: I have been the supervisor for up to five people at one time, and over the past two years have trained 12 people. My responsibilities included teaching company policy to new employees, teaching job responsibilities, helping employees who needed directions on operating laundry equipment, and evaluating workers' performances.

Mechanical Skills: I have repaired industrial laundry equipment when welding, soldering and re-wiring were needed. I have replaced natural gas pipe and have set water pipes.

Learning Skills: Industrial housekeeping requires that workers learn how to operate various types of machinery and how to mix and use various types of cleaning chemicals for different fabrics. I have quickly mastered the knowledge needed in each situation on the job.

(Employment Summary, next page.)

The first page of a Functions Resume.

RESUME

Janice Marie Young
Apt. 24
Holmeswood Apartments
2229 W. 78th Street
Dallas, TX 25235
Phone: (days) 214-555-9927, ext. 1869
(evenings and weekends) 214-555-0401

Career Objective: Market research management in merchandising.

Education: BS in Education, University of Texas at El Paso, 1983.

Professional
Experience: 1985 to present: Employed in the Marketing Department of Holland Department Stores, Dallas. I conduct in-depth interviews with eight randomly selected shoppers per month and write a report for management on the results. I also gather data on competitors from published sources (annual reports, sales promotions, trade newspapers) and write a semi-annual report with recommendations to management. Duties also include reviewing commercial research publications and abstracting information.

1983—1985: Wholesaler's representative to fabric retail outlets. Sold yard goods, patterns, buttons, etc. to store managers. Responsible for setting up displays, collecting from overdue accounts, advising customers on fashion trends outside U.S.

(Summary of Work History on next page.)

Some Words to Help You Describe Your Job Duties

accomplished
achieved
administered
advanced
advised
analyzed
arranged
assisted
audited
authored
budgeted
built
charted
communicated
completed
composed
constructed
conducted
contracted
contributed
created
decreased
defined
demonstrated
described
designed
determined

developed
directed
distributed
edited
eliminated
employed
established
followed through
followed up
forecasted
formed
founded
generated
handled
headed
helped
improved
increased
installed
instituted
invented
maintained
managed
monitored
operated
organized
originated

outlined
oversaw
perfected
performed
planned
prepared
prescribed
presided over
produced
projected
promoted
recommended
refined
regulated
relieved
replaced
reported
researched
revised
served
solved
suggested
superintended
supervised
taught
trained
wrote

Questions and Answers About Your Resume

What is a resume?

A resume is more than a list of facts about you. It is your first opportunity to make a good impression on prospective employers and tell them what is important about you as a worker. Typically, employers are interested in learning why you might be a good person to have on board. What skills do you have? What experience? What record of success or persistence? The answers to those questions should be easily found on your resume.

Suppose I have been working for the last 10 years. All of a sudden I find myself out of work. How do I put together a good resume?

Do an inventory of yourself—what you are good at, what you want to do—and then collect those notes into categories such as education, experience, skills, achievements. You have the heart of a good resume when you have those things down on paper. Be sure to have your resume professionally typed and reproduced.

How much attention does a resume get?

Not as much as you probably imagine. One study showed they got two minutes. Another showed only 45 seconds. Whichever one is correct, the point is you have to look good in a hurry. The information the reader wants has to be easily found. The goal is to get the prospective employer interested enough in your capabilities to want to interview you.

How long should a resume be?

A resume should be only a page or two long in most cases. You need a longer resume only if you are in entertainment, medicine, college teaching or the diplomatic service. In those professions, you tell everything on a resume. In fact, such professions call it a curriculum vitae (Latin for "the course of one's life") instead of a resume.

In some other professions, where it might be important to show the scope of your experience, you can attach lists of what you have done. For example, a writer might put together a standard one- or two-page resume, then attach a list of articles and books published. An engineer might attach a list of projects he or she has worked on.

But remember, most resumes should be short, one or two pages. Almost every employer is going to ask you to fill out an application form, where you can tell everything of any importance.

So the resume is like an advertisement for myself?

Yes, in some ways. It's a no-nonsense, straight-to-the-point ad. It is the way people begin to judge you before they really know you. You are on display in print, so to speak. You'll want to look your best.

How do I choose among the different types of resumes? How do I know which kind to write?

That depends on what is important about you and the type of experience you have. You should choose the type based on what you want to say and which resume will show your skills and experience in the best light.

The old standby, the Chronological resume, is good for almost everyone, but especially for persons who want to show that their work experience has been broad and that they have progressed. On a Chronological resume you might say, for example, that at age 18 you started doing this kind of work, at age 21 you did that kind of work and so on up through the years.

It is a good form to use until you have reached a high level in your particular line of work. Then you should consider switching to something like a Functions resume, an Accomplishments resume or a Special Skills resume.

A Functions resume might be best if you have never had an impressive title. We've all known, probably, the person who virtually did the boss's job but got no credit for it. The Functions resume for Janice Marie Young shows how to handle that. Her title of assistant sales analyst isn't very impressive and isn't mentioned in the description of her work for the department store. The reader sees, though, that she has some important responsibilities. If she had led off with her title, most readers would consciously or unconsciously categorize her as a low-paid clerk. Instead, she emphasized her functions, increasing the likelihood that she will be seen as ready to move up into management.

In the Special Skills resume, you write about the different skills that you have mastered. Maybe you became very good at giving performance and salary reviews to employees, or budgeting, or planning production, or controlling inventory. Maybe you were the best person in the office at getting things done on the phone. Those are all skills that prospective employers might be interested in.

The Accomplishments resume is the Functions resume in the past tense. "Helped bring sales up 72 percent in a period of three years due to a program that I helped devise." Write that way when creating an Accomplishments resume.

Would it be appropriate to consider several different types of resumes for several different types of jobs?
Yes. But don't try to combine all the features of Chronological, Special Skills, Functions and Accomplishments resumes in one document.

The older you get and the more experience you have, the more likely it is that you are going to want to present a different resume to each prospective employer. You will have so many different qualities and capabilities that no single resume will tell the appropriate facts for each job opportunity. Don't hesitate to write special resumes. Match your resume to each job opportunity.

How do I handle the fact that I might not have the right experience for a particular job that I am interested in?
Many successful people have had that problem. Be honest but be positive about yourself. For example, you could tell the employer you have a lot of enthusiasm and a lot of education. Emphasize the interest, enthusiasm and education, and you may find those qualities count for more than experience. Employers know they aren't going to find the perfect candidate every time.

Let's say that I have some gaps in my work record. How do I handle that on my resume and in the interview?
It used to be that gaps in employment automatically meant there was something wrong with the applicant. Now employers are accustomed to hearing that someone took six months off to go to Europe, or a year to help take care of an ill relative or two years to be with a child. Whatever the reason for a gap in your

employment—just couldn't find a good job, poor local economy—recognize it, let your prospective employer see it and deal with it honestly.

Once I have completed my resume, how do I go about getting some constructive criticism about it?

Ideally, you will find some people who have experience in personnel work to review your resume. (Consider, for example, personnel people at a former employer, business teachers, business colleagues). And ask friends or family members to read it. Get all the comments you can from people who either know the hiring process or who know you.

Any final comments about writing a resume?

Don't reinvent the resume. Almost everybody you know has written one. Learn from them. Ask them what worked and what didn't. Ask where they had it typed, where they had it printed. What would they do differently? At the same time you're asking those questions, you are getting your name into circulation. That is a key element in finding the right job.

3
How To Write A Good Cover Letter

Why a Cover Letter Is Necessary

The cover letter is sometimes called a job application letter. Whatever the name, it should always accompany your resume and should always be a personal letter. Don't send your resume without sending a cover letter with it. The cover letter is a personal piece of communication, addressed to someone; a resume is not. The letter is therefore slightly more likely to be read, judged and passed to someone else who is looking for a worker like you.

Address the recipient by name if you can, not by title only. Don't write, "Dear Sir or Madam" or "Dear Dr. Morrison." If necessary, call and ask the name, the spelling and the preferred courtesy title (Mr., Ms., Miss, Mrs.) of the person you are writing to. That is much better than a guess. Anything you can do to get your letter to a person capable of hiring you is worthwhile. Otherwise, your effort—and your chances of getting hired—could go in the waste basket along with ads, announcements and appeals for contributions to the Tricycle Hall of Fame.

What Should Go in Your Cover Letter

When the personnel officers of the **Fortune** 500 companies were asked to agree or disagree with statements about cover letters, here's what they strongly agreed on:

- Good grammar and correct spelling are essential. (97 percent agreed)
- The tone of a letter of application is important. (90 percent agreed)
- Letters of application are welcomed even though there are no jobs open at the time. (89 percent agreed)
- The cover letter and the resume should be typewritten. (88 percent agreed)
- Letters of application should include a reason why the applicant is interested in the particular job. (81 percent agreed)

What statement did they *not* agree with? A cover letter only (no resume needed) gives all information about the applicant. (No one agreed with that.)

They also turned thumbs down on catchy first sentences in letters of application. ("Dear Mr. White: Your company can survive without me but not very well!")

The survey of 200 college recruiters and 25 communications teachers revealed that:

- Most cover letters are quickly evaluated—only those that put across the writer's strong points quickly are fully evaluated.
- Cover letters are usually scanned or retrieved when new jobs open.
- Cover letters should be one page.

The most common reasons for **rejecting** applicants on the basis of cover letters were:

1. Spelling errors.
2. Poor grammar.
3. Poor organization.

4. Little evidence of performance level.
5. Abilities not matched to company needs.
6. Over-emphasis of applicant's needs. ("I am the best so I require your top salary.")

Sample Cover Letters

In most cases, a cover letter has to be only three paragraphs long.

The First Paragraph:
State what position you are applying for, and if appropriate, how you found out about it. ("I am applying for the position of programming analyst, advertised in the most recent issue of **Computer Tech News.**")

The Second Paragraph
This is your "highlights" paragraph. You tell why you are especially suited for the position and what particular talents or experience you have that makes you a good candidate. ("I have an associate degree in programming and two years' experience in programming for an engineering firm.")

The Third Paragraph
This is usually the closing paragraph. Tell the reader that you would like an interview and make it easy for her or him to give you an interview. One way to do this is to offer to set up the appointment. For example, say that you will call a few days after the letter arrives to ask for an appointment. Then make that call.

Sample Cover Letter

104 Drury St.
Bether, KY 86061
December 1, 1988

Harlan Milton, Ph.D.
Director, Hotel Security and Housekeeping
La Place Hotel
11092 N. Main St.
Indianapolis, IN 55622

Dear Dr. Milton:

    I am writing to apply for the position of Housekeeping Manager, advertised in the Sunday Times this week.

    For the past two years I have managed housekeeping and laundry work at the Indiana School for the Blind. My responsibilities include supervising five workers, teaching new employees their jobs, and evaluating their performance. I have a total of five years' experience in housekeeping work and am looking forward to moving into more management responsibility. I will finish work on my associate's degree in institutional maintenance in six months, and I plan to get a bachelor's degree in hotel management soon after.

    I will be calling next Monday to see if a personal interview can be arranged. Thank you for your attention to my application, and I look forward to meeting you.

Yours truly,

Wilson B. Lane

WBL/cm-r

Attached: Resume

Sample Cover Letter

> Apt. 29A
> Cavalier Court
> West Vaca Blvd.
> Fort Deering, NY 10021
> December 1, 1988

Herbert Mendenhall, President
Mendenhall Manufacturing, Inc.
Industrial Parkway
Ringolsby, NY 10023

Dear Mr. Mendenhall:

I am writing to inquire about the possibility of employment at Mendenhall Manufacturing. Bill Sworski, your vice president of finance, told me you were interested in finding experienced people for your expanding marketing operations.

I have nine years' experience in steel marketing: three as a salesman, one as an area sales manager and five as produce manager for coated stock. I feel I know the customer base well and I have several ideas to help you penetrate further the major market segments that Mendenhall serves.

Will you grant me an interview? You can call me evenings and weekends at 555-5344; during the work week, reach me at 555-2000. I have enclosed a copy of my resume.

> Sincerely,
>
> Myron W. Elder

mwe

4
Interviews: How To Get Them And Conduct Them

Finding a Job Opening

When you have defined what you want to do and what you are able to do, you are ready to begin looking for a job opening. Here are some of the best ways:

Friends, social and business acquaintances, members of your professional organizations

The richest source of new jobs is your network of friends and acquaintances. Why? In some cases they have the boss's ear; they have heard about upcoming changes in their company or a competitive company; they know your work and/or your character; they want to do a favor in hopes of getting a favor; they want to show how influential they can be; or they are just kind folks. If they know you, they feel good about recommending you. *Fully 90 percent of the people who successfully find jobs do so because they told someone they were looking.* Get your name out to enough people and someone will likely call and say, "Someone here told me about you. How about coming in for an interview?"

Want ads

Consider *placing* want ads as well as reading them. Besides the want ads in your hometown newspaper, consider using the classified sections of papers in large cities nearby, the newspapers of distant cities that are sold at the local newsstands (*The New York Times, The Wall Street Journal*, for example), and specialty newspapers such as The Wall Street Journal's *National Employment Weekly*. Also read and consider placing ads in the journals and magazines that serve the industry or profession you are interested in (for example, *Ad Age, Automotive News, Psychology Today, Scientific American*). Most public libraries have recent copies. Check their reading racks.

Employment agencies

You'll find them all listed in the Yellow Pages. Agencies come in all sizes and degrees of specialization. Some are highly selective in what type of worker they will look for and what type of employer they will serve. Many do not charge a fee to the person looking for a job; instead, they are paid by the employer. Ask questions. Find which agency or agencies you want to work with. Check with friends to learn what they know about them. Remember, too, some states and cities operate employment agencies.

Headhunters

Depending on your profession, there may be the opportunity to use headhunters...people who specialize in matching individuals to jobs. Headhunters are similar to employment agencies except that they specialize in finding candidates for a particular type of job or profession. Often they tend to specialize in management, executive, high-tech or service types of positions. You can find out who the headhunters are for your profession in several ways: ask colleagues, contact professional associations or watch trade and professional journals. Your initial contact with a headhunter should be in the form of a letter that explains your situation, briefly describes your experience and gives some idea of the type of job you are looking for. Also enclose a resume.

The local business and "old pals" networks

The Rotary Club, the Optimist Club, veterans' organizations, civic booster groups—almost any organization that you or a family member belongs to has some prospective employers in its membership. One reason these groups exist is to help one another in business. You won't be the first or the last to find work through them.

Professional organizations
Secretaries and nurses, firemen and foresters, plasterers and pianists, lab technicians and teachers—all of these and thousands of other groups have professional organizations. Many publish a newsletter or magazine listing job openings. Get on the mailing list if you aren't already. Also, someone at the group's national headquarters is probably the unofficial job broker. Call and ask. They are the job brokers because they like to help.

Your banker, insurance agent, realtor
Persons who are out and about every day in the business world often hear about jobs before they are advertised. They know about construction projects just starting, new businesses moving to town, new government services and proposed bond issues that could mean new jobs. Also, the members of your local Chamber of Commerce have virtually a direct line to employers. You probably know a member of the Chamber or someone who does.

Bulletin boards
These are especially useful to hourly workers and skilled workers. The bulletin boards are found in hardware stores, lumber yards, plumbing shops, glass installers and auto parts stores. If you are looking for work in the trades, check the bulletin boards. Consider posting your work-wanted ad there, too.

How to Get an Interview

When you find a job opening you are interested in applying for, there are several ways you can go about getting an interview.

If you are responding to a classified ad, your first step should be to send the information requested in the ad. If the ad doesn't indicate the employer and you mail your materials to a post office box or a box number at the publication, you will have to wait until the prospective employer contacts you.

If the ad gives the company's name, address and the name of an individual to mail your materials to, then:

- Address the cover letter to the individual indicated in the ad. (Double-check the spelling of this person's name!)
- See if you know anyone who works at the company who can mention your name and your interest in the job to the person reviewing applicants and/or the individual you would be working for.
- Several days after you have responded to the ad, call the individual who is reviewing applicants and reiterate your interest. Ask if he or she needs any further information, and indicate that you would like to schedule an interview where you can learn more about the position and discuss your qualifications.
- If an interview is scheduled, ask if it would be possible for you to pick up a formal job description of the position prior to your interview. If you can, you will be better able to match your skills to what the company needs during the interview.
- Get background information on the company and their products/services before you have your interview. The easiest way to do this is to get a copy of their most recent annual report. You can request this directly from the company or your local library might have a copy. If the company does not issue an annual report, try any sales or informational literature the company might produce on its products/services.

If you hear of a job opening through friends, call the individual who is doing the hiring and explain how you became aware of the position. Very briefly explain why you are qualified and indicate that you would be interested in meeting with him or her to discuss it further. You will probably be asked to send a resume or possibly be told interviews aren't being scheduled yet. With the former response you can follow the steps listed above. If you get the latter response, follow up with a letter that expresses your interest and enclose a resume for their file. Make a note to check back later if you have some idea of when they will be actively looking to fill the position.

Before arranging your first interview, know what your former employer will say about you. Don't settle for, "We'll give you a good recommendation." Ask what will be said about you. You have a right to know and you're not being unreasonable to ask. If you learn that you'll get a poor recommendation, negotiate for a better one. For example, if a former employer says he or she will say you were absent more than five percent of the time, ask him or her to add that it was due to an illness in the family, if that was the case. One way or another, it is best to know what a former employer will say about you so you can deal with the recommendation intelligently.

Find out if the people you list as references object to being listed. (Just alerting them to the fact that they might get a call helps them give a good reference.) Also find out how they prefer to be addressed, what their phone numbers and addresses are. Have that information written down so you are ready to give it on an application form. "He's my minister at the All Pray Church and the number's in the phone book" is very little help to a prospective employer.

How to Conduct Yourself During an Interview

The most important thing to remember is that you never get a second chance to make a first impression. With that in mind the following are essential in interviewing:

- Be on time. Allow extra time for parking, heavy traffic or finding an unfamiliar address.
- Dress appropriately for the position. Even if the position requires you to wear a uniform or dress very casually, be sure to wear appropriate attire for the interview.
- Be organized. Bring additional copies of your resume or any other materials that might be appropriate to show your skills.
- Ask basic questions regarding the job. What is the job description for the position? What are the company's expectations of this individual?
- Look the interviewer in the eye when you are talking and listening. Don't look around the room.
- If you like what you hear and think you want the job, say so. Be enthusiastic and tell the interviewer you think you could do an outstanding job for the company and would like to be given that opportunity. Depending on your style

and that of the interviewer, some prospective employees have been successful by asking "When do I start?" at the end of an interview.

Be Sure to Follow Up After the Interview

You can set yourself apart from other applicants by following up after the interview. Most people don't.

Follow up by writing a short note to the persons you interviewed, thanking them for their time, expressing your continued interest in the position and indicating that you look forward to hearing from them soon.

Be sure and write this note and mail it promptly after your interview (within 24 hours).

Questions and Answers About Interviews

Any general advice about preparing for an interview?

Find friends and family members who will give you a practice interview. Let them ask you all the tough questions and see how well you do. For example: "Why do you want to do this kind of work? What are your qualifications? What do you know about our organization? Why did you leave your last job? How long do you intend to stay with us? Why would you be any better than other candidates?" And urge your practice interviewers to dream up questions you don't expect.

What questions should I ask?

Ask what is appropriate to your interests. Do you want a description of job duties? If so, ask. Sometimes it is appropriate to ask such questions as: "What do you consider the best (and the worst) things about working here?" "What advice would you give someone who wants to work here?" "How might I avoid mistakes you've seen other new workers make?" "Who would I report to?" Very often, answers to those questions come out before you ask. You can also ask about company benefits. Sometimes the questions just don't apply. But think through what you want to know and be prepared to ask.

Okay, what else do I have to do to prepare?
Think through what you will say if you get an offer. Are you ready to discuss salary or wages? What amount do you expect? When are you ready to report for work?

What are the other important things I should keep in mind?
Two things go into first impressions—how you look (posture, clothes, manner, mood) and how you speak. Many young people, especially young women, speak too softly in business situations. They don't want to be brassy or crude. But your ability to make yourself understood is important in most jobs and certainly important in an interview. You have to be able at least to communicate what you know. Look your listener in the eye, speak clearly. If you find you're being interrupted often or getting smiles in the wrong places, it might be because you are speaking too softly.

Interviewers typically want to know what you know about their organization. Your knowledge and interest make a difference. You make a good impression when you know about their company. Find out what they do and how they view themselves. Are they strictly a "lowest-price" outfit? Proud of their community work? Dedicated to finding new products? Read their quarterly and annual reports, or ask to see company literature ahead of time. Employers can only be interested in people who are interested in them.

What other kind of research can I do if I am interested in a particular company or industry?
Networking is one of the best ways. Go to someone that has worked for that company or is working for that company now. Ask a friend to ask a friend who works there. Use your network of acquaintances not only to find out about a company, but to get your name circulating there as an employable person.

How about interview scheduling?
Arrange at least one interview a week. This has the advantage of keeping you active, keeping your name out there and keeping you feeling that you have something to look forward to. If you let a week go by without one, you might settle into a comfortable but bad habit. You can start losing self-confidence and self-respect, and that may come across in future interviews.

When companies have a job opening, how do they go about recruiting for the position?

Walk-ins get a lot of the jobs. Depending on the type of job, some people just drop by and ask to fill out an employment application. This is not a good idea if you are interested in a management or supervisory job or many positions above entry level. Also, companies take applicants from the past month or two and review them for prospective employees. Generally it is assumed that if you submitted an application or resume more than a month or two ago you have already found a job. If good candidates aren't found this way, then companies generally advertise.

Let's say that I was let go from my last job—I had a negative experience. Should I wait for the interviewer to bring it up or should I talk about it first?

Whatever you feel comfortable with; however, if you can bring up and discuss this issue comfortably, it can be an opportunity to demonstrate your honesty, maturity and professionalism.

If I have been out of work for a few weeks, is that a special concern to an employer?

Not necessarily. There are all kinds of circumstances that might lead to that. Maybe you have been searching for a job and just haven't been able to find a good one. Explain your situation if asked, but don't be apologetic.

Is it a good idea to take a temporary job while I'm looking for one I want to keep?

It can be, but it depends on the job, how long you've been unemployed and your financial need. You have to weigh the benefits, financial and psychological, of working versus the fact you will have less time to search for the permanent job you really want. Advantages to temporary jobs are: regular income, possibly health benefits and the opportunity to enhance existing skills or help you gain new ones. The disadvantages are: less time to devote to job hunting, the perception by a prospective employer that there may be some problem that makes you unhirable (raises the question, "If he's so good, why hasn't someone hired him yet?"), and the tendency to get stuck in a "temporary" job.

If I didn't get the job that I interviewed for, is it ever appropriate to call that employer to find out why?

Certainly, to improve your interviewing techniques, if nothing else. Maybe you presented your education and training wrong. Perhaps you didn't make clear that you had a lot of experience. You have to find out so you can do better on the next interview—and you might re-awaken the interest of the company that turned you down. When asking this question, avoid being apologetic, angry or frustrated. Your approach should be professional, and the purpose of your call should be self-improvement.

5
Tips On Filling Out An Application Form

Not many of us can remember all the dates, names and addresses called for on employers' application forms. We need some help, such as the practice application form on the following pages. Fill it out at home, at your leisure, where you have such things as your address book, the phone book and records of your previous jobs to help you. This form is similar to the ones used by most employers.

Remember, employers want all the information requested. They may think you're hiding something if you leave blanks.

When you've finished filling out the practice form, take it with you to help you fill out actual applications.

PRACTICE APPLICATION FORM

PERSONAL INFORMATION

Date _____ Social Security Number _____

Name _____
      Last   First   Middle

Present Address _____
          Street   City   State   Zip

Phone No. _____ Height _____ Weight _____

State name and department of any relatives, other than spouse, already employed by this company. _____

Referred By _____

EMPLOYMENT DESIRED

Position _____ Date you can start _____ Salary desired _____

Are you employed now? _____ If so may we contact your present employer? _____

Ever applied to this company before? _____ Where _____ When _____

(Continued on next page)

EDUCATION	Name and location of school		Circle Last Year Completed	Did You Graduate?	Subject Studied And Degree(s) Received
Grammar School				☐ Yes ☐ No	
High School			1 2 3 4	☐ Yes ☐ No	
Trade, Business or Correspondence School			1 2 3 4	☐ Yes ☐ No	
College or University			1 2 3 4	☐ Yes ☐ No	

Subjects of special study or research work _____

What foreign languages do you speak? _____

What foreign languages do you read? _____ Write? _____

Activities other than religious
(civic, athletic, etc.) _____
EXCLUDE ORGANIZATIONS, THE NAME OR CHARACTER OF WHICH INDICATES THE RACE, CREED, COLOR OR NATIONAL ORIGIN OF ITS MEMBERS.

(Continued on next page)

FORMER EMPLOYERS List your last four employers, starting with the last one first.

Date Month and Year	Name and Address of Employer	Salary	Position	Reason for Leaving
From				
To				
From				
To				
From				
To				
From				
To				

REFERENCES: List the names of three persons not related to you whom you have known at least one year.

	Name	Address	Business	Years Acquainted
1.				
2.				
3.				

(Continued on next page)

PHYSICAL
CONDITION: Do you have any physical condition which may limit your ability to do work applied for?

_____

In case of
emergency notify _____   _____   _____
                       Name   Address   Phone No.

I authorize investigation of all statements contained in this application. I understand that misrepresentation or omission of facts is cause for dismissal. I understand and agree that my employment is for no definite period and may, regardless of the date of payment of my wages and salary, be terminated at any time without notice.

_____   _____
Signature   Date

6
How To Stretch Your Money To The Max

Depending on your situation, a major part of the stress associated with looking for a job can come from financial pressures. Here is a discussion on how to make the most of the money you have and how to find resources you didn't know you had.

What steps should I follow when I find myself without a job?

First, you need to assess your financial situation on paper, even if writing it down reveals a picture you don't like. There is less anxiety in knowing than there is in ignorance.

Write down your assets and your debts, your monthly income and all the monthly or weekly expenses you can identify—all the financial realities you have to deal with in the coming weeks or months.

How do I set up a personal budget? Where should I start?

Go to any bookstore and pick up a household budget book. This makes it easy to list all your various expenses—rent, gas, electricity, groceries, that kind of thing. You will not only see how much you now spend every month but where any waste is.

Suppose I find I have more bills than I can pay?
Talk to your creditors. Generally, creditors will work with you if they understand what your problem is. They have little to gain by not cooperating with you. Fill them in on your financial situation. Don't hold back out of embarrassment. Usually they want to come to some kind of terms on how to pay your obligations. Offer them specific alternatives such as partial payment, extended terms, etc.

What about credit cards?
Credit card issuers should be handled as fairly and openly as other creditors.

In many cities you'll find a name such as Credit Counseling Service listed in the phone book. Many such services are run by not-for-profit groups such as churches or city government. You might be pleasantly surprised at the professional help you can get in managing credit card accounts and all your other credit obligations.

How do I deal with unreasonable collectors?
A collector can reasonably expect you to tell him or her when you are going to pay your bill. He or she can't be abusive or harass you. He or she can't call you at odd hours or at work if you tell him or her not to. The law provides a lot of protection. Answer collectors' questions, but don't put up with abuse. You don't have to.

Do I have more financial resources than I realize?
Yes. Most people don't know what their net worth is. They are surprised to learn that they have money in the cash value of a life insurance policy, for example, or maybe some money in a company pension plan they can utilize.

Other possible sources of funds: back pay, severance pay, unused vacation pay, partial year's bonus, expense account balances, profit sharing.

What are some good belt-tightening techniques?
Keep track of every penny you spend. If you put a quarter in a candy machine, jot it down so you know what you spend. After you keep records for a week or more, you will discover that you are spending a lot on things that you don't need.

What about the really big items, like mortgage payments?
If you are paying on a mortgage and money is really getting tight, check into paying just the interest each month. Your mortgage holder will give you details, but often you can make the interest payment only and suffer no consequences except having your payments stretched over more months. For example, many mortgage holders will still give you a good credit rating if interest but not principal is paid on schedule.

7
How To Handle The Stress Of Job Hunting

There is no doubt that not having a job produces stress. If you are worried, acknowledge the fact and then put it aside. Let friends and family help—without wearing them and yourself down with negative emotion. Channeling your emotional energy—and time—into useful action is the key. The following discussion gives some insight into the process.

Suppose it is Monday morning or the day after graduation and I find myself without a job. What should I do?
Begin by examining your feelings about the situation; give yourself a moment to acknowledge them. Then ask such questions as:

- Was my last job beyond my capabilities?
- Was it outside my interests?
- Did I enjoy the work?
- Did I have control of circumstances?

Then get organized. Define your career objectives, write your resume and start job hunting.

Many people feel they have lost their identity if they don't have a job. How can I prevent that feeling?
Work gives us much of our sense of identity—particularly our professional identity. This is because work is such goal-oriented behavior. We find out who we are, in work terms, when someone tells us we are doing well or doing poorly, when we get paid, when we are missed if we don't show up, when we are praised for doing something special. We are always getting some kind of feedback on the job, so it is enormously important in how we think of ourselves. Take that away and you lose a huge chunk of your self-image.

Avoid slipping into this mind-set by getting support from your family, friends and professional associates. Also remind yourself of your skills, your assets and your accomplishments. Finally, try to see this process as a new opportunity which will allow you to achieve even greater things in the future.

Suppose I am starting to feel that finding a job is hopeless. How do I deal with that?
It is easy to get discouraged if you've had numerous interviews, sent out dozens of resumes and are still jobless. However, hopelessness is a terminal disease to someone seeking a job. It makes them incapable of projecting interest and enthusiasm or even discussing their past accomplishments in a positive light with a prospective employer. If you feel hopeless, express it privately to friends and family members. Get support from these individuals. When you go for an interview, regardless of how bad you feel, you have to change your attitude. If necessary, pretend you are an actor and the interview is your stage. Your character is competent, enthusiastic and fully qualified for the job in question. Use whatever tricks are necessary, but express your negative feelings at home and leave them there.

How do I turn the panic associated with looking for a job into the power I need to find it?
The key issue here is the ability to control your attitude. If you let panic overwhelm you, you will not be able to muster the confidence and energy you need to get a new job. There is no doubt that regardless of how good you are at controlling your attitude, you will still have moments of panic. It can be an excellent motivator. But let panic be only that: a motivator.

Finally, the reason you panic is because you are afraid you won't be able to find the job and the salary you want. The likelihood of this happening is very small *if* your expectations are realistic, your job definition is fairly flexible (you can't set your sights on just one company), your experience and skills are in line with the job you want, and if you work diligently and persistently at the *job* of finding a job.

SPECIAL HANDBOOK OFFER

Buy two, get one free!

Each of our handbook series (*LIFESTYLE, COMMUNICATION, PRODUCTIVITY* and *LEADERSHIP*) was designed to give you the most comprehensive collection of hands-on desktop references all related to a specific topic. Plus at the unbeatable offer of buy two, get one free, you can't find higher quality learning resources for less! **To order**, see the back of this page for the entire handbook selection.

1. Fill out and send the entire page by mail to:

In U.S.A.	In Canada
National Seminars Publications	**National Seminars Publications**
6901 West 63rd Street	10 Newgale Gate, Unit #4
P.O. Box 2949	Scarborough, Ontario M1X 1C5
Shawnee Mission, Kansas 66201-1349	

2. Or ***FAX 1-913-432-0824***

3. Or call toll-free ***1-800-258-7246*** (in Kansas, 1-913-432-7757)

Fill out completely:

Name _____
Organization _____
Address _____
City _____
State/Province _____ Zip/Postal Code _____
Telephone ( ) _____

Method of Payment
☐ Enclosed is my check or money order
☐ Please charge to:
 ☐ MasterCard ☐ Visa ☐ American Express

Signature _____ Exp. date _____
Credit Card Number

To order multiple copies for co-workers and friends: **U.S.** **Can.**

20—50 copies........................$8.50 $10.95
Over 50 copies........................$7.50 $ 9.95

LEADERSHIP

Qty.	Item #	Title	U.S. Price	Canadian Price	Total Due
	410	**The Supervisor's Handbook, Revised and Expanded** The nation's resource on supervision. A must for today's effective supervisor.	$12.95	$14.95	
	458	**Positive Performance Management: A Guide to "Win-Win" Appraisals** Learn to create a strong, comprehensive review system.	$12.95	$14.95	
	459	**Techniques of Successful Delegation** Get more done through others with lasting results.	$12.95	$14.95	
	463	**Powerful Leadership Skills for Women** Become the effective leader your employer needs!	$12.95	$14.95	

COMMUNICATION

	413	**Dynamic Communication Skills for Women** Enhance your promotability with effective communication skills.	$12.95	$14.95	
	460	**Techniques to Improve Your Writing Skills** Write effective reports, letters and memos with powerful new techniques.	$12.95	$14.95	
	461	**Powerful Presentation Skills** Discover the doors to career advancement that powerful speaking can open.	$12.95	$14.95	
	482	**Techniques of Effective Telephone Communication** Impact your organization's bottom line with professional, polished telephone skills.	$12.95	$14.95	
	485	**Personal Negotiating Skills** Learn the art of negotiating with all types of people in a variety of situations.	$12.95	$14.95	

PRODUCTIVITY

	411	**Getting Things Done: An Achiever's Guide to Time Management** The ultimate approach to managing time and priorities.	$12.95	$14.95	
	483	**Successful Sales Strategies: A Woman's Perspective** Increase your sales success with strategies that get results!	$12.95	$14.95	

LIFESTYLE

	484	**The Stress Management Handbook** Get more enjoyment out of every day with proven stress-reducing techniques.	$12.95	$14.95	
	486	**Parenting:** *Ward and June Don't Live Here Anymore* Get tips for handling your most common parenting challenges.	$12.95	$14.95	
	487	**How to Get the Job You Want** Turn your goals and ambition into a satisfying, rewarding career.	$12.95	$14.95	

Subtotal	
Special 3-book offer (U.S. $25.90; Can. $29.90)	
Kansas residents add 5.5% sales tax	
Shipping and handling ($1 one item/.50 each add. item)	
TOTAL	

Thank you for your order!